Praises, Prayers and Promises

By

Jenny Miller

PROISLE PUBLISHING

Praises, Prayers, and Promises

Copyright © 2022 by Jenny Miller

ISBN: 979-8-9867806-5-8

All rights reserved. No part of this book may be reproduced or transmitted in any form or by any means, electronic or mechanical, including photocopying, recording, or by any information storage and retrieval system, without permission in writing from the copyright owner.

The views expressed in this work are solely those of the author and do not necessarily reflect the publisher's opinions, and the publisher disclaims any responsibility for them.

To order additional copies of this book, contact:
Proisle Publishing Services LLC
1177 6th Ave 5th Floor
New York, NY 10036, USA
Phone: (+1 347-922-3779)
info@proislepublishing.com

I began drafting a few poems when I was fifteen, like most young wishful girls. I knew I had a talent for writing poetry. But later, I got bored with friends, school, work, and dances. Life got in the way. I put my poems on hold for a long time. Then I had children, which made me want to write again. But I still was not serious about it; after quite a few years, I re-dedicated my life to Jesus; even though I was saved when I was twelve. At this time, the poems came flowing; the Lord gave me these words. I hope this poem collection will bless you and bring you comfort and closer to our Heavenly Father. I hope you let them fill your heart with hope and gladness. Use them when reading your Bible to help give you hope along the way. They are for every occasion and event, from birthdays to Christmas. From weddings to funerals or whatever the occasion may be. I pray they will carry you through your days, whatever they may be.

Blessed is the man that walketh not in the counsel of the ungodly, nor standeth in the way of sinners, nor sitteth in the seat of the scornful. But his delight is in the law of the LORD; in his law doth he meditate day and night.

Psalms 1:1, 2 KJV

Dedication

I dedicate this poem book to the Lord for The beautiful gift he has given me. I have been through heartbreak, severe illness, and the loss of loved ones. And only with the Lord have I been able to weather the storm. I thank God for bringing my husband to our Savior, Jesus Christ. God has made my life whole and beautiful and has given me grace. I thank my Lord for my children and grandchildren for the blessing they bring. I thank my husband for the love he has given me. For the strength, he has shown and the kindness and patience. You have been my pillar and have always shown me what love meant. I thank you for being there through thick and thin and marrying me. Thank my children and grandchildren for your love, laughter, and smiles. I cannot be prouder of all of you. You have and always will be a wonderful tribute to the happiness the Lord can bring a person. Thank you to my sister, who listened as I shared my poems and scriptures. I hope they will be a true blessing in your life. Thank you to my brothers, who I know always loved me.

Table of Contents

Prayer.............................. 1
A Babe.............................. 2
A Song.............................. 3
Angels.............................. 5
A Soldier's Parent's Prayer........7
A Man Called Jesus.................9
A Psalm Promise....................11
Anger..............................13
Creation is........................15
Cry................................16
Dearest Lord.......................17
Do I Have a Choice?................18
Faith..............................19
Friends............................21
Gentlemen Cowboy...................22
God is There.......................23
Happiness..........................24
Happy Birthday.....................25
Healing............................26
Lasting Happiness..................27
Life...............................28
Loss...............................30
Mist...............................31
Mother, Mother.....................32
Mother.............................33
My Prayer to You...................35
Ode to a Life......................36
Ode to a Valentine.................38
Our Fortress.......................39
Prayer.............................40
Prayer for Women...................42
Remember...........................43
Seeking Faith......................45
Song in my Heart...................46
Stay...............................47
The Forest.........................48
The Gift of a Child................50
The Good Shepherd..................52
The Great "I Am"...................54
The Lord is my Shepherd............55
The Potter and the Clay............56
The Promise........................58
Trust..............................60
Understanding......................62
What a Wonderful Thing.............64
What Is a dad?.....................65
What is a daughter?................66
What is a Friend?..................68
What is a Husband?.................70
What is a Memory?..................71
What is a Woman?...................73
When God Created a Mother..........75
You................................77
You Are............................79

Prayer

I thank you, God, for your gift so true,
God in Heaven hears me pray as I go about my day.
That each person be blessed and guided by you,
And feel uplifted the whole day through.
Please help those in need or who walk alone.
I pray these poems will make them feel at home.
Within the hearts of their family and friends,
Are they close or making amends?
Please, Lord: bless all those who read,
Give them a gift and help those in need.
Thank you, Lord, for all those who hear and see,
Your love is in action in the words we read.

I thank my God for making mention of thee always in my prayers
Philemon 1:4 (KJV)

I have always found it easy to pray for anything. It does not matter what time of day or what I am doing, and I know the Lord can hear me, and he always answers my prayers. My prayers have carried me through some of my roughest times and have made all the special occasions more memorable.

A Babe

He came as a babe in the middle of the night.
In a time when the world was full of hate and strife,
Ears fell upon the call of this child.
Which came to heal the sick and the lame.
The stars are shown brightly in the heavens above.
The word of His coming and God's great love.
Came to the many who would believe,
This babe would someday lead.
Those out of bondage from sin and shame.
The wise men, the gifts of love for this child, came.
He then carried a cross that our life would not end.
Ears heard of this extraordinary deed.
For our sins, He did bleed.
He is a beacon and our light.

John 3:16 (KJV)
For God so loved the world, that He gave His only begotten Son, that whosoever believeth in Him should not perish, but have everlasting life.

It is effortless to say the prayer when you take Jesus as your Savior. It is not a lot of work, just a simple prayer, and you will be saved and go to Heaven someday.

PRAISES, PRAYERS, AND PROMISES

A Song

The Lord put a song in your heart; it is a song to sing.
It will give you a lift and give you a ring.
For others who hear and sing along,
The Lord will help make you strong.

A song to sing is a beautiful thing.
It can make you cry; it can make you dance.
Just think of what it can do by chance.

Sing a song and sing it well,
The Lord makes it easy as ringing a bell.
It is a song; it is a story that is to tell.
It will put a spring in your step,
It is a poem; it is a thought.
It can be a feeling that sends you reeling.

The Lord put a song in the heart; it is a song to sing.
That kept you smiling and keep you feeling.
A song in the heart is a song from God indeed,
He will give you a lift when you are in need.
God put a song in your heart for all to see.
He put it your heart and soul where it needs to be.

The Lord put a song in your heart; it is a song to sing.
It puts a spring in your step and gives you a ring.

I will be glad and rejoice in thee: I will sing praise to thy name, O thou most High.

Jenny Miller

Psalms 9:2 (KJV)

I sing in our church choir, and I come from a family that played music together.

Music puts a song in my heart; it always has a story to tell and gives everyone a message.

It is always uplifting when you hear music or sing, especially if you are singing praises to the Lord. He will also bless you when you sing your praises to him. My uplifting moments are when I sing or listen to music that puts a song in my heart.

Angels

Each new day passes in this world we call life.
There are promises of angels when our steps turn into strife.

We may never know when our paths may cross.
This may be your friend, family, or boss.

In any season, there is a reason.
Look close at this person on good days and bad.
Or it may be when you are feeling sad.

When someone is called home from afar,
Or, in each step, we take or drive a car.

The time will come when you need a lift,
God blesses you with a gift.

Do not take for granted the person next to you,
It could be an angel from the heavens blue.

I know this to be true; I have seen it in my family
And you will too.

When standing in line or just crossing the street.
Life is unique, and the day is sweet.

No matter when, even if they are good days or bad days.
In the days of bitterness, or when the end is near.
Let us not forget or fuss.

We are walking among Angels.
And angels are walking among us.

My grandmother and mother, and sister are my special angels. And I believe we all have special angels that bless our lives in one way or another. Some we may never see again, others may live next door, or they may be right in your home and family. I always try to remember that I could also be that special angel to someone. I once met a woman who helped me in desperate need. I had been praying that God would send someone to help me, and there she was. I have never heard from her since, so the Lord does send angels into our life.

He shall give his angels charge over thee, to keep thee in all thy ways.
Psalms 91:11 (KJV)

A Soldier's Parent's Prayer

May my prayer go out with you today?
With all the lost soldiers, so long is the way.
Gone, but never forgotten,

They will be remembered as little boys at play.
I give this particular message.
To the many who are the few;
The Lord keeps you safe and sound
As you fight for freedom on the ground.
He will keep you in his care,
Even if you are in the heavens, he will hear your prayer.

You have the wings of angels now,
And no more sweat on your brow.
Calm the hearts of loved ones as
They mourn the loss of their daughters and sons.

I pray that those who are still in the fight,
The Lord is with you through the night.
He will keep you in his care,
When walk where eagles dare.

Thank you all for what you have done,
You are our daughters and our sons.

My sons served in the military and were glad to defend our county. Then after September 11th happened, my youngest Son was called to Iraq. He did two tours while there; his wife had two children, one of who was sick. My

Jenny Miller

Son could go home for this, and he had to return as soon as she was out of danger. I know what it feels like to know that your child is fighting for our country. I felt proud, worried, prayed, and looked forward to the letters and calls. As I know, my Son also looked forward to those calls and letters. I was lucky enough to have my Son survive the war. He and his wife now live in the same town as me, and I have three grandchildren!

And take the helmet of salvation, and the sword of the Spirit, which is the word of God.

Ephesians 6:17 (KJV)

A Man Called Jesus

God sent a man called Jesus to this Earth.
This took place as a virgin birth.
In his life, he never took a wife.
Instead, he told of God's word, and everyone heard.

He was forgiving and kind and never sat in any pews.
Only wanted all to believe; all they had to do was ask.
He was hung on the cross because of this task.

To this day, he is here for us.
No matter if we're on a bus, we only need to pray,
Ask him to come into our hearts to stay.
Then from here on, the joy will start.
What could be easier than this to tarry?
This man called Jesus had the cross to carry.

When in doubt and are not sure.
Remember the thief was next to him who was pure.
He was forgiven because he believed.
Of whom God told Mary he would be conceived.

All you must do is pray, ask, and believe.
What could be more wondrous and unselfish?
But this man called Jesus who walked this Earth.

God loved us all, so he sent us his only Son,
So, he could die on the cross so all would not be loss.
How could you not believe what he has done?

As you read this poem, you will know.
Ask someone who believes; they will show.
Who is this man is on the cross and bare our sin?

    I feel very humble when I read about this incredible man that once walked our Earth. When I ponder about Jesus, who came to this Earth as a man. I find it more than my mind can comprehend that he came from Heaven and was able to perform all the miracles. But at the same time, I know he is my Savior who gave his life for my sins so I would have everlasting life. That someone could love me so much that they were willing to put their life on the line. As a parent and grandparent, I would give my life to save theirs. I wonder if this is how God felt about His Son.

For thou, Lord, art high above all the Earth: thou art exalted far above all gods.
Psalms 97:9 (KJV)

A Psalm Promise

Joy in the strength of our Lord,
in thy salvation, he gives us a sword.

Give us blessings of goodness,
Well done, good servant,
The promise of a crown on our head,
For making him most blessed.

Trust in the Lord with all you might,
He shall not be moved in the darkest of the night.
He restores my soul; blessings will follow the rest of my life.

Dwell in the house of the Lord forever and ever, Amen.
He gave us his Son so that we may live again.

This is his promise to those who will hear
The lamb's voice, whether it be far or near.

The Lord is not fussy, but he is coming back.
You will not join if you do not hear.
It is your life that he bought.

In the time of doubt, take heed,
it is Him that you need.

I trust the Lord; he has always carried me through the thick and the thin in my life. I know I am here today only through my trust in Him. Have you ever heard the saying, "That's a promise, not a threat?" This is what I thought of when I drafted this poem. The Lord meant every word he said in the Bible. It is not just a story; it is his Psalm Promise of what he will do.

I will say of the Lord, He is my refuge and my fortress: my God; in him will I trust.

Psalms 91:2 (KJV)

Anger

Anger is a feeling we do not understand
It can be with anyone, a child, a woman, or a man.
We do not always know why we feel this emotion.
God gave this to us; it is like being in the ocean.

It can be on the spur of the moment, the loss of someone close.
It can be from an event, not something that we chose.
We do not always follow what our heart is telling us.
We go with the anger instead.

Ask what caused this terrible feeling.
Where do I go from here?
Use our fist or shout or just leave it alone.
It is better than saying nothing.
If we do, we can never go back home.

Anger is not just an emotion; it is a feeling near.
It is a feeling that everyone does fear.
Just pray to God he will hear your voice from afar.
Do not keep your anger bottled up in a jar.
Talk to anyone who will listen.
It is better than being sorry and crying boo hoo.

This poem is in the book I wrote, Remembering When. I wrote it to explain to others how anger made me feel. Sometimes I did not even know what it was; I was angry about it. There were times when I found that I did not even know that I was angry. As the poem reads, do not keep your anger bottled up in a jar. Talking about it is the best thing to do; when someone is listening and caring, it helps you to see that you are not alone. It is better than being sorry because your judgment of things is not as clear when you are angry. So, you make wrong choices and could end up doing damage to others or yourself.

Cease from anger and forsake wrath: fret not thyself in any wise to do evil.
Psalms 37:8 (KJV)

Creation is...

Creation is the heavens that are so blue.
Creation is a flower that softens with the dew.
Creation is...
Creation is the trees that whisper with the wind.
Creation is the Spirit that dwells deep within.
Creation is...
Creation is the mother whose babe has been born.
Creation is the mother whose love is not forlorn.
Creation is...
Creation is the Lord, who worked for six days,
He rested on the seventh.
Creation is...

In the beginning, I drafted this poem when I was fifteen. I was in school when a teacher confronted me and said that this poem was good enough to be published. Here it is now in a book for everyone to read. The Lord truly creates the loveliest things.

In the beginning, God created Heaven and the Earth.
Genesis 1:1 (KJV)

Cry

I will cry tomorrow,
No matter what the cause.

I will cry tomorrow,
When I hear the trumpets come.

I will cry tomorrow,
No matter what the loss.

I will cry tomorrow,
And when all is said and done.

Jesus' gift is an eternal one,
So, if I put off today, what
I know I should have done it.

I will cry tomorrow.

When I think of this poem, I remember what the Bible says. I drafted this poem to remind me that there is a more significant loss than that of my life here on Earth. And I need to show compassion for the ones I love and those I meet. It reminds me to not put off important things and to enjoy every moment of every day.

And shall not God avenge his elect, which cries day and night, though he bears long with them?
Luke 18:7 (KJV)

Dearest Lord

You know and understand all things.
You know that someone special.

Have they just lost a loved one? They need strength and comfort now.
Please surround this dear friend with your loving presence...

Guide each step of the road ahead,
By your grace, grant them faith that brings peace of mind.
In the heart, with the hope that washes all sadness away.
In the days ahead, the sweet memories will fill the loss instead.

It came to pass, the angel of the Lord spake these words unto all the children of Israel, that the people lifted their voice, and wept.
Judges 2:4 (KJV)

The Lord is very dear to my heart when in times that I am alone or with others; I always know he is my dearest Lord. He is my strength and comfort; when someone is hurting over a loss of a loved one, it is good to know that we can always turn to God. I always remember that everything is in God's timing and does everything out of love for us. Although we may not always understand how he could take someone we love so dear away from us. I try to remember that they would have suffered dearly if they had survived. Or they would be unable to live life to the fullest as we want them to.

Do I Have a Choice?

My first commitment of the day to take.
Is a call I have to make.
Listening to the ring, waiting for an answer, it is a recording.
The voice on the end sounds as accurate as can be. Oh, I see; to my surprise, I am given a choice, an authentic-sounding voice telling me to make a choice of numbers or a name, a song to sing.
It is all about waiting to be connected, for Heaven's sake.
When suddenly there is a sound, it is music I hear, not a voice; what happened?
To my surprise, I am put on hold. How can this be?
I hit the pound sign on the phone, hoping to be connected to a person.
Please, please, grant me patience, Lord but hurry.
I pace the floor. I pray again. Lord, give me what I need; I hit the zero key.
I called to get the info; I do not wish to take too long.
I will not take up your valuable time.
Please do not tell me this is wrong.
I wait and wait while I listen to a song.
Make a choice, I am told, or choose an extension.
I just need someone to listen.
Here my please, don't you see?
I started this call in the morn, and now I am forlorn, for it is nigh, oh my!
Hello, hello, is that you? This is me!
Then what is it that I hear, oh, dear!
I panic; this is not my plan.
Can this be? I do not know what you're saying to me.
What is your name?
I begin to talk and try to explain when I hear music again, to my disdain.

Faith

What is faith?
Is it the substance of things we do not see?
Or the things we hope to be.
What is faith?
Is it something real or something we feel?
Could it be the look on someone's face?
It is the gleam in their eye or just a place.
What is faith?
Who is the finisher of our faith?
Is it here on Earth or in Heaven above?
Is it a babe's birth?
Could it be flying as a dove?
What is faith?
You put your faith in men that do not win.
Do you put your faith in something not seen?
It could be somewhere that you have been.
What is faith?
You get put to the test daily.
That is when you know where your faith is.
Do you know what you believe is true?
Pray to God and read his word,
Then it will give you a clue.
Do you know what faith is?

I drafted this poem because my faith has seen me through the most challenging times in my life. It has been

Jenny Miller

faith that has kept me singing and being able to hold my head high no matter what was going on. I have always kept my faith no matter how dark or dreary the path I took was. I could not have done it and would not be here if it were not for my Lord and Savior, Jesus Christ.

Now faith is the substance of things hoped for, the evidence of things not seen.
Hebrews 11:1

Friends

A friend is someone who listens and cares.
Helps when you need it when no one is there.
The best gift of all is a friend for life.
A confidante and ear to heart in the middle of strife.
One who is for you no matter the time,
Sometimes like a lemon or lime.
If when sour, add a little sugar; they are tasty and sweet.
A friend like this just cannot be beat.
If you're looking for a friend, see within yourself,
Add a few qualities of unselfish giving.
Love, understanding, and forgiveness are what a friend is after.
Be sure to include a lot of laughter.
There will be tears to share and jokes to tell.
Take care, my friend; say a daily prayer.
God will bless you and take care after.

Proverbs 18:24 (KJV)
...A man that hath friends must hew himself friendly: and there is a friend that sticketh closer than a brother...

I have great neighbors who are also my friend. I consider my spouse, brothers, and sisters my friend.

Jenny Miller

Gentlemen Cowboy

Gentleman cowboy,
Where have you been all my life?
The Lord gave your love to me.
You are what I have always dreamed of.
I yearned for you in my years of strife.
The Lord blessed me as your wife.

Gentleman cowboy, gentleman cowboy,
You are mine and mine forever.
My love for you is vital; it gets stronger every day, every minute.
With love like this, it will not die-no, not EVER!

Gentleman cowboy, now your heart is mine.
The Lord blesses and keeps us, here now always, till the end.

I wrote this after I met my husband. I gave this to him in a card on our first anniversary. He reminded me what true love for someone is. When we first met, he opened doors for me and had me walk on the inside of the sidewalk when we walked together. He said his mother taught him to be a gentleman. It is important to always let someone you love know how you feel. I do this best by writing about it; my grandmother always told me to give flowers while they were here.

And the servant of the Lord must not strive; but be gentle unto all men, apt to teach, patient
2 Timothy 2:24 (KJV)

God is There

When in a time of turmoil, remember God is there.
He knows what you need and listens to your prayer.
In times of trouble or triumph,
Call out to Him in time of despair.
It does not matter when or where.
Ask, and He will show you how with care.
It is as easy as calling out or picking up a phone.
It does not matter if you're away or at home.
He really does answer and leads you out of trouble.
Keep your faith in Him no matter what or where you are.
God is never very far.

Psalm 34:4 (KJV)
I sought the Lord, and He heard me and delivered me from all my fears.

When in doubt, I always pray. I know God hears me because peace flows through me. And I feel at ease.

Happiness

To say, "I Love You." to say, "I Do."
It is not too many; it is only but a few.
Who finds special meaning?
And to think it is you two.

This is to say congratulations and best wishes too,
That God in Heaven will bless you with a long life of happiness.

I am so happy to say, "It is about time you two tied the knot,
Before you became known as the ones that time forgot!"

I wrote this for a couple I was close to and had waited a long time before getting married. I wanted it to be uplifting and funny, but at the same time, I wanted it to be a blessing. To know it is enough to love for each other to say, "I do."

I delight to do thy will, O my God: yea, thy law is within my heart.

Psalms 40:8 (KJV)

Happy Birthday

Happy Birthday is a way to say, "I love you."
It makes you older every year; age is a number.
It does not put us asunder.

The Lord gave you a particular day.
You are as young as you feel,
You are so very, very real.
Happy Birthday is what I am trying to say.

You are a person in your little way
; it is for laughter, a day for play.
Happy Birthday is what is what I am trying to say.

I wish you happiness throughout the year.
This greeting is sent from afar or near,
stop and listen with your ear.

You are sweet in your little way.
Happy Birthday is what I am trying to say.
The Lord blesses and helps you have a wonderful day.

Happy Birthday, we all want to wish those around us this wonderful message. It is not just another day of growing older; it is also a milestone in our life to know that we have yet lived another day. On the day we were born, we were very loved. Not just by our parents but also loved by God.

For whom he did foreknow, he also did predestinate to be conformed to the image of his Son, that he might be the firstborn among many brethren.
Romans 8:29 (KJV)

Healing

Is remembering when a part of the healing?
It is something that sends you reeling.
When you are sitting in your chair,
Coming to terms with what is there.

What it is that is on your mind,
Could it be sad or something kind?
You feel the fight within your heart,
When what you know is honest from the start.

Bruises you feel and ones you cannot see,
Start to fade and begin to heal,
You know where you want to be.
It is a better place for you and me.

Part of healing is mourning the loss of innocence from a broken heart. And God promises that he heals all wounds, and with faith, we will grow stronger and become whole again.

Psalm 147:3 He healeth the broken in heart and bindeth up their wounds.

Lasting Happiness

To say I love you to say I do.
It is not too many and only a few. Who finds special
meaning to think it is you?
Who have a love for each other like no other?
Congratulations and best wishes too.
Celebrate the years as they come,
On a long life of happiness.
When taking your vows and tying the knot.
Before becoming known as the two, that time forgot!

Genesis 2:24 (KJV)
Therefore, shall a man leave his Father and his mother, and shall cleave unto his wife: and they shall be one flesh.

I hope this poem will give you a little laugh and inspiration. This verse was read to us when I married my husband. God has blessed us with many years together, and our love for each other is due to Him.

Life

I am tired of this thing called life.
The news and the gossip we tend to read.
I am tired of the newspaper stories they bleed.
We believe what we hear and see.

Do we know what it is we need?
I am tired of the daily grind.
The things they hold and the things they bind.

I have my coffee and my cereal bowl,
I get on my way just like before.
I am tired of this thing called life.
The job the drive the traffic takes its toll.

At the end of the day, I drive to my door,
There to greet me is my wife, just like before.
I realize what I am doing this for.

It is not just for me or my job, nor the bills I pay,
Nor the house I live in from day to day.
So, when I get tired of this thing called life.

I think of my lovely pregnant wife.
What a precious gift God has given me,
It makes all my days more worthy for me to see.

When what we know is somehow, someday.
He will take care of the business.

Praises, Prayers, and Promises

Why wait till tomorrow for what you can do today?
Take Jesus as your Savior; He will pave the way.

You will live in gladness with a song in your heart.
There will not be any regret or doubt about your choice.
You will just wish you had done this from the start.

Go to the Lord in prayer today.
Do not put it off; there may not be a someday.

Sometimes we all get tired of living with the stresses of the day, things that can go wrong. Mistakes we can make and accidents that can happen. But I always remember to turn to the Lord in prayer. It always uplifts me and helps me to know that I am not alone. Taking him as my Savior has given me strength, and having the Lord in my life has made it more abundant.

For what is a man profited if he shall gain the whole world and lose his soul? or what shall a man give in exchange for his soul?
Matthew 16:26 (KJV)

Loss

In a time of loss,
There is nothing to gain.
It is a time of solitude, sorrow, and pain.

We have our fears, and we pray in gratitude.
Our loved one has Heaven to gain.

We want God to hear our plea for forgiveness.
When what we know is somehow, someday.
He will take care of business.

Why wait till tomorrow for what you can do today?
Take Jesus as your Savior. He will pave the way.

You will live in gladness with a song in your heart.
There will not be any regret or doubt about your choice.
You will just wish you had done this from the start.

Go to the Lord in prayer today.
Do not put it off; there may not be a someday.

It does not matter what kind of loss you have. There are different kinds of loss, including a loss of a loved one. Going through a divorce or a lifelong friend moving away. No matter how you look at it, it is a loss. But take care in knowing there are others you can turn to that have known loss too. Get in prayer to the Lord. He will help comfort you and show you how to overcome your loss.

And when he cometh home, he calleth together his friends and neighbors, saying unto them, rejoices with me; for I have found my sheep which was lost.
Luke 15:6 (KJV)

Mist

A glowy fog that lays low to the ground, but anyone it will not bind
God made this weird stuff without sound.

If you walk out far and lie down.
There is not one who will find you or take you away.
The Lord will help you not to stray.

I assure you; that you will not be bothered if you just stay.
The Lord made this part of the day.

Have you ever looked at fog? It has a hypnotic calming effect. Do you see the wonder of God's creation? It is not just fog; it has moisture in it. The dictionary defines it as; Fog is a collection of liquid water droplets or ice crystals suspended in the air at or near the Earth's surface. I do not look at it scientifically; only God could make something so stunning.

But a mist from the Earth went up and watered the whole face of the ground.
Genesis 2:6 (KJV)

Jenny Miller

Mother, Mother

Mother, Mother, there is no other.
She gave me life because of God above.
She taught me to make like a dove,
to learn, laugh, and love.

Mother, Mother, there is no other.
So humble and giving her love divine.
She gave me hope; she gave me praise.
She gave me wishing wells all my days.

Mother, mother, there is no other.
She helped me when I worked and toiled.
She was there when I was troubled.
She taught me well so that I may learn.

She passed from this life; she left a legacy that I may earn
Strive for the best and not give up.
Mother, mother, there is no other.
I was fortunate to have her here on Earth.
The memories live long and will not fade.

My mother passed when she was just sixty years old; she was like a sister to me. But there is nothing like having a mother.

My Son, hear the instruction of thy Father, and forsake not the law of thy mother:
Proverbs 1:8 (KJV)

Mother

Mother is the one who gave us life from God above.
She taught us to fly like a dove, to learn to laugh and love.

Mother, there is no other,
So humble, giving her love divine.
She gave us hope; she gave us praise.
She gave us wishing wells in our days.

Mother, she helped us when we toiled.
She helped when we were troubled.
She taught us well that we might earn.
She left a legacy that we would learn.

Mother, she passed from this life she loved very much.
She wanted us to strive for the best to not give up.
To be able to say I want that somehow someday.

Mother, there is no other.
She gave us a sister or even a brother.
So, we would have someone to share and grow with.
To share our fears, tears, and stories.
She taught us to give God all the glories.

Mother, she is now in Heaven above.
Her star shines; you can see it glow.
It is the brightest one that you choose and know.
You keep her favorite cup,
And have coffee every morning in her honor.

Mother, there is no other.
God gave us this gift, and he took her home.
Now the stress and strain in her life will not bother her.
There is no other; she is now with her sister and mother.

Mother, there is no other.
Keep her close to your heart and treat her with tender care.
For we never know how long she will be here.

These poems are a tribute to my mother and mothers everywhere. When my mother was called to Heaven, I knew the only way I would keep her close was in memories. I hope that all women can be close to their mother while she is on Earth.

Honor thy Father and mother; (which is the first commandment with promise.
(Ephesians 6:2 (KJV)

My Prayer to You

The Lord has truly blessed us,
Of good friends that always cheer.
Whether they are far or near.
They are so pleasant and warm to be around.
They are not just friends.
They are the family we have found.
This is my prayer to you,
You will be in God's grace
And it will keep you safe.
He will pave the way for you to go.
Whether you are young or when you are old.
So, keep a prayer in your heart
And know that this is my prayer to you.

I wrote this as a prayer to everyone, hoping it would encourage and uplift you. So, you would know that you are never alone. Someone is always praying for you, so the Lord will bless you and keep you safe.

Give ear to my words, O Lord, consider my meditation.
Hearken unto the voice of my cry, my King, and my God: for unto thee will I pray.
Psalms 5:1-2 (KJV)

Ode to a Life

His love for life was just that,
With his family by his side,
He lived his life far and wide.

His love for life was just that,
He was able to fulfill his list,
Through love and strife,
For the wishes of his family,
He made a promise to return and hug his loving wife.

His love for life was just that,
The Lord carried him through,
He soared in the wild blue,
Over the ocean, he flew.

His love for life was just that,
Every dream was fulfilled,
He survived the most, and
Lived to be a part of all,
That God leads him to.

His love for life was just that and more,
He leaves his memories and all his love,
He is up in the heavens now soaring as a dove.

His love for life was just this; there is a difference now.
He is better than he was; now, he is made new.
He made a promise of life for many but the few.

Praises, Prayers, and Promises

Ode to a Life is a story for anyone to know God is here for you. Do not put your trust in men; they will not always be around. God is always there, no matter where you are or what you do. *He said he would never leave nor forsake us.*

My righteousness I hold fast and will not let it go: my heart shall not reproach me so long as I live.
Job 27:6 (KJV)

Jenny Miller

Ode to a Valentine

"Who was to know when you proposed to me,
On bended knees, we would still feel the same way.
As this story to you shows."
When we met, it was fate?
With the first kiss, I felt unsure; it was our first date.

I was positive there was something amiss. But you were strong and assured me you were here to stay. Years Have passed since we were married,
We showed true love does not stray.

We have seen death, illness, and many major surgeries.
We still show our love, as God has blessed us from above.
We now have grandchildren, and as we grow older, there is no regret.
It still feels like when we first met.

It is lovely to know when it is all said and done,
That true love can happen to anyone.

I love you to the man in my life.
Happy Valentine's Day from your loving wife

One of my favorite holidays is Valentine's Day. The hearts, the love, and the flowers always give me a warm feeling to know there is so much love to give. It is one of the most expensive holidays for giving flowers and candy. What a sweet way to show love and to provide a card from the heart.

And I will give them one heart, and I will put a new spirit within you, and I will take the stony heart out of their flesh, and will give them a heart of flesh:
Ezekiel 11:19 (KJV)

Our Fortress

God made the beginning; He made the end.
He made it so we may lend an ear of His mercy.
It stands His word forever so true.
Then we may go and tell someone like you.
Jesus is our fortress; he is excellent and just.
We are to enjoy what He gives us if we do not lust.
His love for us is much. There are quite a few who
Will you not hear of any of the great miracles of him?
The Bible is His open word
We can read and use it as our sword.
He loves all mankind. He loves everyone.
We pray we believe, and we accept what God has done.

My friends and family would always look to me because of my strength. I was asked, "Where do you get such power?" My reply is, "The glory goes to God, and without him, I would not have the strength he has given me."

And he said, The Lord is my rock, and my fortress, and my deliverer
2 Samuel 22:2 (KJV)

Prayer

Prayer is a beautiful thing.
It's singing praises to a King.
It lifts you and puts a smile on your face.
It warms your heart; it makes you want to sing,
"Amazing Grace."
God will see you through prayer, heart, and soul.
It makes a grown-up cry and a child sigh.
God created the skies of blue.
It is like His word; it is true.
Prayer, it is in me; it is in you.
We need to pray if it is only a few.
Just bow your head, and tell God what you need.
It may not be when we say.
However, God might answer right away.
When in doubt, say a prayer, and keep your faith.
In addition, show God you care.
Prayer is telling God what you need.
It is as easy as sowing a garden and planting a seed.
So, say your prayers through the day.
Say a prayer at night and from the start.
God will be there for you every day, everywhere.
Moreover, it will put a song in your heart.

Prayer is an essential part of my daily life. It is communication with our Lord. I get strength from it, and it gives me faith to face another day. Prayer has never failed me; many have been answered. I prayed for fifteen years that my husband would accept Jesus as his Savior. Three months after starting to go to church with me, my husband took Jesus into his heart. We are now Sunday school teachers. There have been several other answered prayers in my life as well.

Evening, and morning, and at noon, will I pray, and cry aloud: and he shall hear my voice.
Psalms 55:17 (KJV)

Prayer for Women

Dear Heavenly Father,
Watch over these women today,
Keep them safe as they go along their way.
Let them know you are with them in times of struggle.
And give them warmth when they want to snuggle.
Help them with their duties they stave.
With the knowledge you so graciously gave.
I love these women, and thank you, Lord,
Please pour your blessings upon each one,
So, they will be able to bless others too.
As they say their prayers and give glory to you.

I drafted this poem when I gave a message to the women at my church. The Holy Spirit moved me that these women needed special prayer. My heart goes to women everywhere; you are the handmaiden of the Lord. You raise the children he blessed you with and a mate to your husband. We all have expectations of ourselves, and this prayer will always be there for you.

But thou, when thou prayest, enter into thy closet, and when thou hast shut thy door, pray to thy Father which is in secret; and thy Father which seeth in secret shall reward thee openly.
Matthew 6:6 (KJV)

Remember...

God bless you as you,
Remember when, as a little girl?
When were you playing freely with a twirl?

God bless the fragile and innocent, so little time spent.
There was nothing serious, just everything quaint.
A flower blooms in the spring with a delicate scent.
With their petals soft and fragile,
Holding and cherishing them as if they were medals.

Remember when, as a young teen, to dream?
While thinking about every moment, with the excitement of a new dream.
Worry about hair, nails, and things. These were the biggest of tasks, it seems.
God gave you these beautiful things.

Remember as a young woman of twenty?
A job, a date, the dream of marriage,
The task at hand was listening to the ocean,
In the seashell found,
On the beach, in the sand,
Remember as a woman of thirty?
The trials and tributes of motherhood,
The wonder of life, as you learned the meaning,
God gave you a child of your own to watch, grow, and mature.

As you remember what it was like,
Be in awe of such a wonder.

Remember these things and hold them, dear, to your heart,
These things God has blessed,
And in your mind, they will never part.

    I drafted this poem when I decided to write my first book about the abuse my mother and I went through growing up. I say this because my mother was only sixteen when she gave birth to me, so, in essence, we grew up together under abuse. We did not get to experience everything this poem says about a girl and/or a woman.

For I will be merciful to their unrighteousness, and their sins and their iniquities will I remember no more.
Hebrews 8:12 (KJV)

Seeking Faith

It is not faith in a man you understand,
When you want a helping hand.
God is near. Have faith He will give you what you seek.
No matter how small, large, or grand and bleak.
Man of the world is needful making mistakes and taking its toll.
Faith abounds and is always full.
Keep your faith; it will make you strong.
You will hear and sing; what will it bring?
As with a promise, this is true.
Like the heavens are blue.
It is a live thing you have in God.
It is as simple as giving a nod.
Faith goes a long way; man will last for a stay.
Faith in man or trust in God?
It is your choice, like growing grass or sod.
Which one will be greener?
God is peace; keep your faith in what you desire.
See which one will bring you higher.

Proverbs 20:6 (KJV)
...Most men will proclaim every one his own goodness; but a faithful man who can find?

As I have dictated to others. I have always tried to keep my faith, knowing that God will always carry me through each day and trial. Staying faithful to His word and living a good life, I have found guidance and direction.

Song in my Heart

There is a song in my heart for You, Lord.
I got a song in my heart for you,
You make my day in every way.
I got a song in my heart for you, Lord.

I cannot stop thinking about you, Lord.
You saved me in every way.
I got a song in my heart for you, Lord
I got a song in my heart every day.

There is a song in my heart for You, Lord.
It makes me smile, and it makes my life.
It does not matter where I am or what strife.
I got a song in my heart for You, Lord.

My days are filled with the glory of You, Lord.
Every day the sun shines in my corner for You,
I cannot stop singing; my ears are ringing,
I got a song in my heart for You, Lord.

I always have a song in my heart after I have spent time in his word and praying. I was sitting in church when the inspiration came to me for this poem. It is so incredible how the Holy Spirit speaks and gives inspiration to what the Lord wants us to speak, write or sing about.

Let the word of Christ dwell in you richly in all wisdom, teaching and admonishing one another in psalms and hymns and spiritual songs, singing with grace in your hearts to the Lord.
Colossians 3:16 (KJV)

PRAISES, PRAYERS, AND PROMISES

Stay

You have made your way into my heart Lord.
    That is where I want you to stay.

You make me laugh; you make me sing.
    You help me to say such beautiful things.

You are my best friend and my true love.
    You are on my mind every second of the day.

You have made your way into my heart Lord
    That is where you will always stay.

Many times in my past, when I asked someone I grew close to if they would just stay around. But that is not how life is, so we must let go and hope we will see them again someday. But there is one thing I know for sure I will never have to ask the Lord to stay. He promised everlasting life and said he would never leave nor forsake us.

My heart is fixed, O God, my heart is set: I will sing and give praise.

Psalms 57:7 (KJV)

The Forest

Are you too close to the forest to see through the trees?
It is what I have been told when people have these.
The doubts when you talk you will not believe.

If you are too close to the forest to see through the trees.
Do you do what you want even when it is wrong?
Would you climb the Empire State Building like King Kong?

When you are too close to the forest to see through the trees,
You know what is right but still do not listen.
Are you still trying to find out what it is that is missing?

When do you know you are too close to the forest to see through the trees?
You do not leave the hive alone when getting stung by bees.
You are stubborn, but it is your body you must appease.

Why are you too close to the forest to see through the trees?
You can be happy as can be; it will depend,
The choices you make will show.
Do you go through life with guilt in tow?

No, it is not natural forests was talking about here.
There are no squirrels, rabbits, or deer.

It is a thing called life
; it is as easy as getting married
or saying, "I do." when you take a wife.

Too close to the forest to see through the trees.
It is all about choices; it is easy as a breeze.
You just need to step back, listen and be,
What is someone trying to help you see?

I am often called upon by my friends and relatives for advice. But it never fails when I give it or try to help them see their situation more clearly. They are just too close to step back and take a look at what the problem is. They do not want to accept that things around them need fixing. So that is where I thought of this poem.

And he shall be like a tree planted by the rivers of water, bringing forth his fruit in his season; his leaf also shall not wither, and whatsoever he doeth shall prosper.
Psalms 1:3 (KJV)

JENNY MILLER

The Gift of a Child

He came in the middle of the night,
The world was full of hate and fright.

Ears fell upon the call of this newborn,
Who came to heal the sick and save the forlorn?
The stars showed brightly in the heavens above.
All knew of the word of His coming because of God's great love.

He came to the many who would believe.
That this babe would someday lead.
Those who are trapped, the lost and weary,
Out of bondage or out of sin and shame.
The three wise men the gifts of love
For the child, they came.

He then carried a cross,
That our life would not end.
Ears heard of this beautiful deed,
How for our sins did he bleed?
He came as a babe in the middle of the night,
That he could be a beacon and our guiding light.

I not only look at this child that came to Earth as Jesus. I also look at the wonder of his birth, and the time it came to be. What Mary and Joseph must have felt seeing this baby and knowing that he would grow up and be a king and die for their sins and everyone! How proud they must have been to know this. It is the same with you and me; we are in awe of this wonder when we have a baby. We are proud and grateful that the Lord gave us such a wonderful gift.

And she brought forth her firstborn Son, wrapped him in swaddling clothes, and laid him in a manger because there was no room for them in the inn.
Luke 2:7 (KJV)

The Good Shepherd

Verily, I say unto you,
I come to the door and knock.
I am not a stranger that you should lock.

All that came before were robbers and thieves,
He calls his sheep by their names and leads them out.

Verily, I say unto you beware of the day
And hear the shout the time is near.

He is the good shepherd, and he answered and said,
I am a man called Jesus' my sheep I have led.

Verily, I say unto you,
Come to the altar, and you will be fed.
You will not see death,
You will have nothing to dread.

Verily, I say unto you,
Do the good deeds come to be true?

He is the Good Shepherd,
You will grow and love.
He sent His promise in the form of a dove.

A good shepherd, my brother-in-law grew up around sheepherders. And my husband helped on ranches with sheep. He told me how stupid sheep are, which is why they need a sheepherder. Sometimes we can be foolish and stubborn, which is why we have the Lord as our shepherd. Not that he looks at us as stupid, but he knows our thoughts and every move we make. He wants us to turn to him not just when we feel lost but always.

I am the good shepherd, and know my sheep, and am known of mine
John 10:14 KJV

Jenny Miller

The Great "I Am"

I love this world; I love this land.
Most of all, in the heavens above,
I love the great "I Am."

He gives me strength and shows me the way.
He gave me Jesus and taught me to pray.
He hears my prayers and answers them.
Without my Heavenly Father, I would not be where I am.

So, when I am looking around at the beautiful site,
I know I will forever keep my eyes on my Heavenly Father.
And my heart and mind on my Savior, Jesus Christ.

He is sometimes called the precious lamb,
I will always know him as the great "I Am."

When Moses stood on hallowed ground and asked God, "Who will I tell them that sent me?" I have always known that our Lord is the great I am. From the time I first saw a movie about Jesus dying on the cross for our sins to the time I took him as my Savior. Nothing will ever be more significant than, The Great I Am. He has answered so many of my prayers and blessed me with the beautiful life I have now.

And when I saw him, I fell at his feet as dead. And he laid his right hand upon me, saying unto me, Fear not; I am the first and the last.

Revelations 1:17 (KJV)

The Lord is my Shepherd

The Lord is my shepherd,
He guides me to witness and tell.

The Lord is my shepherd,
He showed me His love on the cross.

The Lord is my shepherd,
He is my Savior; I will not be lost.

The Lord is my shepherd,
He watches me from above as a dove.

The Lord is my shepherd,
I will not cry out, "What's this about?"

The Lord is my shepherd,
Who is blessed of all?
He will cause Satan to fall.

The Lord is my shepherd.
When I pray, I hear his voice as I often do.
I know this poem, and his word is so true.

The Lord is my shepherd.
I drafted this poem when I was in church as the Holy Spirit moved me. He is our shepherd to lead us the way so we can live abundantly filled lives with joy and love. He wants us to know his Son Jesus Christ so we can have happiness and live life to the fullest. He has blessed me with so many things I cannot begin to number them all.

The Lord is my shepherd; I shall not want.
Psalms 23:1 (KJV)

Jenny Miller

The Potter and the Clay

Thank you, Lord, in every way,
Thank you again, Lord, for making my day.
You gave me life abundantly, so
Others could see the potter who made the clay.

My Lord is loving, faithful, and kind.
He is not here on Earth but in my heart.
He has been there from the start.

How I know this is through the faith,
He lives abroad and in Heaven blue.
I know someday I will be there too.
Thank you, Lord, in every way,
Thank you again, Lord, for making my day.

He is strong. He gives me this to say,
He will save you from sin if you let me in.
He gave life so all ears could hear,
The love He gave how very dear.

To trust in Him is the place to begin.
Thank the Lord in every way,
Thank Him for making this day.
He will make your life more abundant.
So, you can tell others about the potter and the clay.

When I think of how the Lord made Adam and Eve, the Lord took the dust and molded it as an artist does with his clay. I think of how we are miraculously born as a baby here on Earth and how the Lord also developed us while we were in the womb. And how he gave me a mouth to breathe and talk so I could show everyone he is the potter and the clay.

But now, O Lord, thou art our Father; we are the clay, and thou, our potter; and we all are the work of thy hand.
Isaiah 64:8 (KJV)

The Promise

The Lord hates braggers unless they are bragging on him.
He is selfish but in a beautiful, loving way.
He loves humility, so we might see.
The way of life he wants us to be.

He gave us his word that we would not perish.
He showed his love so we would cherish it.
The Lord wants all to know.
He sent his Son because he loved us so.

The Lord hates sin: it ruins lives if you let it in.
He made a promise to those who believed,
He will return, so we will cleave.
Not on this Earth but in Heaven above.
He gave life to show you his love.

The Lord made a promise to you and me.
He gave his word for all to read.
Come to the Lord, give your sin to bear.
You will find out what it is to care.

The Lord hates sin, but he loves us all.
Do not make a mistake, do not be misled.
The Lord is faithful, and he is not dead.
Come to him who labor and hurt.
He will give you rest,
He will save you from thirst.

Praises, Prayers, and Promises

Read the Bible, and you will see.

Have faith in him and let it show,

The way you live is for all to see.

 A promise is when you say something you intend to do or keep all of your life. It is not something you decide you do not need to keep anymore. I have promised my husband to stay married to him no matter what. When my children were born, I promised to always love them no matter what, just like the promise I made to God that I would follow him no matter what. I intend to keep the promises I make here on Earth.

Preserve me, O God: for in thee do I put my trust.
Psalms 16:1 (KJV)

Trust

It was the worst day of my life when I lost my pride.
I had no one to why is this happening, I cried.

I knelt on my bended knee and began to pray.
I asked God to show me.
How do I take things in strife to show me the way?

He tried, but I did not want to hear
I did not want to see it.
He took my pride, but He stood by my side.

He told me great stories. I then began to cry.
Please help me to be that which I cannot see.

What must I do to get a helping hand?
With the things I cannot understand.

It is God's will against mine.
I was to learn in time I cannot stand alone.

Just because I think I can.
I must trust in the Lord, not in man.

What do you put your trust in? I have asked that question several times, and the answer I get is I am unsure. I know what I put my trust in, and that is God. He has and never will fail me from when I had brain surgery to when I almost lost my Son. I wrote my first book when we were so poor we had to live in a camper for a year. The Lord has always been there because I put my trust in him.

As for God, his way is perfect; the word of the Lord is tried: he is a buckler to all of them that trust in him.
2 Samuel 22:31 (KJV)

Understanding

To understand is to be there,
When watching this woman and this man.

To understand is to be there,
To see the children so innocent,
So precious to do what they can.

To understand is to be there,
When seeing the pain and the sorrow.

To understand is to know,
When there may not be a tomorrow.

To understand is to know,
You can always run away.

To understand is to find you,
Will not face harm another day?

To understand is to pray,
Have faith; it will bring answers.

To understand is to know,
God is there to help you carry on.

To understand is to know,
Each new day brings a new dawn.
Do you know what it is to understand?

I understand that I have rules to follow and am

PRAISES, PRAYERS, AND PROMISES

obligated to raise my children in a loving, safe home. I know when I read something what it says and what the outcome of the story I am reading is supposed to be. But I wonder about all the people who do not know what it is to understand who God and Jesus are. I took Jesus as my Savior when I was twelve. It was a tremendous change in my life. God gave us his only Son so we would have an abundant life. That when we die, we will go to Heaven instead of hell. That is what I understand.

The heart of him that hath understanding seeketh knowledge: but the mouth of fools feedeth on foolishness.
Proverbs 15:14 (KJV)

What a Wonderful Thing

A wonderful thing full of love, hugs, and kisses.
As they become Mr. and Mrs.
The two will join to become one happiness this will bring with a never-ending gold ring.
Showing the love between these two,
With the roses and ribbons of blue.
Two people, two lives, and a baby in the midst of this.
Happiness will become of all this bliss.
God created till death doth you part,
It is true love from the start.
Bless this union, God, I pray,
May it grow and flourish day by day.
Marriage, what a wonderful thing.
These two people walking in grace.
Bless it with each day they face.
Most of all, fill them with forgiveness in the years it will bring.

Song of Solomon 1:15 (KJV)
Behold, thou art fair, my love; behold, thou art fair thou hast doves' eyes.

I love being married; we have had our ups and downs. Sometimes we had to learn forgiveness and accept each other's faults. We overlook our mistakes, and I always remember the vows we took and the love we have due for God.

What Is a dad?

What is a Dad?
He is a man that is not at all so bad!
He is the Father of our house,
And he is My mamma's spouse.

He is my daddy, but he does not
Play golf or carry a caddy.
He likes to hunt; he is very blunt.
He is kind and sweet.

His second favorite thing to do is eat.
His first is to hunt geese or hunt for deer,
Then give a big cheer!
What is a dad?
I have already told you, but remember, he is not bad.

I drafted this poem because I loved my dad very much. He was very abusive and never saw me as the daughter I wished he saw. I hoped he would get to read this someday, but he never did. A dad is someone you are supposed to look up to and admire. Someone who will make you feel safe and loved. Just like my heavenly Father makes me feel safe and loved.

And call no man your Father upon the Earth: for one is your Father, which is in Heaven.
Matthew 23:9 (KJV)

What is a daughter?

A daughter is someone,
That looks good wherever she goes.
God gave her good looks and eyes of blue.

A daughter is someone,
Who cannot wait for a pajama party?

A daughter is someone,
That loves a mother very much.
She is eager
And has a loving touch.

A daughter is someone,
When a mother says, "It is time to hang up,
You have talked long enough."

A daughter is someone,
Who comforts her mother?
She is the girl who loves God
And makes Him part of her life.

A daughter is someone,
Wondering when she is old enough to date,
She leaves behind memories with haste.

A daughter is someone,
Who has memories she will never forget?
The day a cake did bake,

PRAISES, PRAYERS, AND PROMISES

Just to leave the mess for mom to take.

A daughter is someone,
Well, if you have one or not,
You should know by now.
A daughter is someone.

There is a saying, "A daughter is a daughter all of her life. A son is a son until he takes a wife." This poem is not just for a daughter. It is also for a daughter-in-law because she is also my daughter that the Lord brought to me. She is married to my Son, to who I gave life; he is a special gift from God. This makes her even more special because of her love for my Son. She has blessed us with her presence and has given us beautiful grandchildren. She is just as much a daughter as my daughter is a unique gift that no one can copy or imitate. She also gives me grandchildren and her sweet hugs and cheery smile. They both have a way you can see, hear, and feel.

She girdeth her loins with strength and strengtheneth her arms.
Proverbs 31:17 (KJV)

Jenny Miller

What is a Friend?

A friend is someone who listens and cares,
They help when you need it since no one else is there.
The best gift of all is a friend for life,
She is a confidante, an ear to lend in the middle of strife.

One who is for you no matter the time?
Sometimes like a lemon or lime
If they are sour, add a little sugar, and they are tasty and sweet
A friend like this just cannot be beaten.

So, if you are looking for a friend to see within yourself,
Add a few qualities of unselfish giving,
You will begin to see what the meaning of living is.

A little love and understanding, forgiveness, and
a little understanding that is all a loyal friend are after.
Be sure to include a little laughter.

There will be tears to share and jokes to tell.
Be careful, my friend, say a prayer daily,
God will bless you and keep you well.

I have had a few friends that liked to hang out, go shopping, and just spend time together. There is a saying that you know who your friends are when you are in a crisis. And usually, in my life, no one is there when I need them.

Praises, Prayers, and Promises

But I have had only one true friend here, my husband. I have one other faithful friend, but he is not of this Earth but alive and my Savior Jesus Christ.

A man that hath friends must shew himself friendly: and there is a friend that sticketh closer than a brother.
Proverbs 18:24 (KJV)

Ye are my friends; if ye do whatsoever, I command you.
John 15:14 (KJV)

What is a Husband?

He is a man like God intended him to be.
He is strong and the leader of our house.
He is my spouse, can be funny, even joke around.
He does not mind when I shop.
He takes me out on the town.
He has strong arms to hold me tight.
His promises are for keeps and mean what he says.
He raises our kids, and marriage is his resort.
He takes pride in his work and is loving and kind.
When I tell him there is a honey-do, he sees it through.
He takes things in stride on your heart; he does glide.
A husband is what God made him be.
He is someone who wanted to marry me.

Genesis 1:27 (KJV)
…So, God created man in his own image, in the image of God created he him…

Husbands are to love their wives and treat them with kindness. My husband does treat me with respect and compassion, and he is an excellent example of a husband.

What is a Memory?

Is a memory a fond dream, a happy thing?
The place you went,
A vacation spent.
Someone closes someone near.
A face a smile because someone went the extra mile.
Is it in a second or one hour?
It is something that stays in your mind,
Or does it stay for an hour?
It can leave you; it can be a loss.
It is very precious at any cost.
When the damages were done,
It leaves you feeling you are one.
Is it short or long?
Do you forget, but others stay?
It can be a good one, or it can be wrong.
The brain is a puzzle, a computer,
Things when erased, you cannot copy.
Something from the past,
We remember again.
Something so precious, a memory,
It even remembers when you are in pain.
One thing is for sure we all share this,
An awesome God in Heaven, he gives us bliss.

I drafted this poem because when I had to have brain surgery, I lost my short-term memory. And I had to work hard to remember other things in my life. We experience memory loss when we get older or are under great stress. But there is one thing my troubles have never been able to erase: my Heavenly Father and my Lord and Savior Jesus Christ.

> *Thy name, O LORD, endureth forever; and thy memorial, O LORD, throughout all generations.*
> *Psalms 135:13 KJV*

What is a Woman?

A woman is someone,
She puts God first in her life,
She holds herself high,
While she walks with shining grace.
She always loves to share,
You can see it on her face.
She is a little girl who plays house with a twirl.
She wants to be a mother of a little girl.
She is a teenager who laughs and talks.
She dreams of being a princess in beautiful towers.
She likes to be on the phone for hours.
She is the big sister that cares very much.
She is the one that will go with you on walks.
She is my best friend; she hangs on every word.
She is the shoulder to cry on; she hears every word.
She is the wife that stands by her man.
She is the mother who will put band-aids on everything she can.
A woman is someone God put here on Earth.
He put wings on her back to carry a babe, so she could give birth.
He put a halo on her head to guide her in every way.
She is the one who reminds her children to pray every day.
She is you and I; just look in the mirror, and you will see.

Jenny Miller

We all know what a woman is. But my poem institutes the very inward of a woman. Her thoughts, the tenderness, the softness, and the love she can show and give unselfishly. The Bible tells us there is a virtuous woman, the kind I want and can be. The Lord is a work in me to be able to be the woman he wants me to be.

Who can find a virtuous woman? For her price is far above rubies.
Proverbs 31:10 (KJV)

When God Created a Mother

When God created a mother,
He made her heart pure as gold.

When God created a mother,
He made her heart solid and bold.

When God created a mother,
He gave her a story that would never be untold.

When God created a mother,
He made her agile and created in her life so fragile.

When God created a mother,
He made her hair, that of an angel, soft as silk.

When God created a mother,
He made her skin the color of milk.

When God created a mother,
He made her like no other.

When God created a mother,
He made a miracle that produces miracles.
That is why God created a mother.

This poem is to show there is a particular purpose God has for all mothers. I stand in awe of the creation God made when he made me. I can carry a human inside me. I can go through the worst pain anyone can and still live to have an extraordinary life to hold in my arms. How can anyone question that our God did not create a mother?

Jenny Miller

> *She perceiveth that her merchandise is good: her candle goeth not out by night.*
>
> Proverbs 31:18 (KJV)

You

Do not give me dreams.

Do not promise me things.

The Lord knew what he was doing.

Showing our love, we have two rings.

My feelings are yours.

Your feelings are mine.

That is how the Lord wants it to till the end of time.

How is it we two happened to meet?

The Lord walked us side by side as we took our seats.

We laugh, and we play.

We get serious in our little way.

The Lord is with us all day.

You are my love; you are my light.

You are my sparrow in its short flight.

Always remember it is the Lord who gave us insight.

To be together all our life.

You are mine, and mine to hold

It is God's word that will be untold.

I originally drafted this poem as a love poem for my husband. And it shows our love for each other and the love I hold in my heart for him. I give the glory to God for such an extraordinary kind of love he has given my husband and me. He also said we should give ourselves to each other just like he did with his only Son; he showed the greatest love.

JENNY MILLER

His name shall endure forever: his name shall be continued as long as the sun: and men shall be blessed in him: all nations shall call him blessed.
Psalms 72:17 (KJV)

PRAISES, PRAYERS, AND PROMISES

You Are...

The sweet smell of the flowers in spring.
The dew on the grass in the early morn.
Like the wings of a butterfly that flutters,
She beats her wings as she hovers in the hot sun.

You are my gift from God above,
He made you wise and gave you the gift of love.
The first time I met you was when I was a newborn babe.
The warmth of your touch

Like the trickling spring in the early summer heat.
The ocean is filled with tiny jewels that sparkle and shine.
It makes the whitewash with bubbles which makes it fun.

The wings of a hummingbird are soft, feminine, and fragile.
You are the flower that springs so soft and sweet.
The person I know I always wanted to meet.

You are the person to who I would always go when needed.
You taught me to sew to greet with grace.

You are my grandmother and mine to hold
Your story will become untold.

My grandmother was one tough cookie. She was wise beyond her years; besides my mother, she was the most loving person I could have ever known. She quilted, sewed, canned her food, baked, cooked, and worked in the fields. I drafted this poem for her when I sent her a birthday card for her 65th Birthday. I wanted her to know how much I love her. She was like a second mother to me. I thank my Lord for giving her to me.

She maketh herself coverings of tapestry; her clothing is silk and purple.
Proverbs 31:22 (KJV)

I thank the Lord for giving me the Holy Spirit to write and reach out to others. The Lord wants us to tell others about what he has in store for us. About what kind of love and life he can only give. Through these poems, I hope you will feel and want to have the Lord in your life to help guide you as he has my family and me.

www.ingramcontent.com/pod-product-compliance
Lightning Source LLC
LaVergne TN
LVHW010600070526
838199LV00063BA/5024